SEZ

(Everything Speaks)

Marcus Smith

LIVE CANON

First Published in 2015
By Live Canon Ltd
www.livecanon.com

© Marcus Smith 2015

978-1-909703-07-0

Edited by Helen Eastman for Live Canon

www.livecanon.com

www.marcussmithpoetry.com

SEZ

(Everything Speaks)

Marcus Smith was born in Oxford, raised in America and splits his time between London and the US. He has received prizes, commendations, awards and nominations from Poetry on the Lake, The Pushcart Prize, The Nation/'Discovery' Prize, The Plough Prize, The Ledbury Poetry Festival, The Torbay Poetry Festival, Atlanta Review's 10th Anniversary Anthology, Envoi anthologies, New Millennium Writing Awards, The Thomas Hardy Society, Vers Poetry Society, The Nottingham Poetry Competition and Southern Poetry Review and been featured on The Poetry Shed. Twice a finalist for the Cinnamon Press Book Competition and twice shortlisted for the Bridport Prize, he has published in *Ambit, The Rialto, PN Review, The Shop, Able Muse, Ploughshares, Poetry Salzburg Review* and has been a stringer for *New Musical Express*.

Acknowledgments

Portions of *SEZ* have appeared in *The Text* and *Recours au Poème*.

'I saw your name' appeared in *The Rialto*. '58 Dead In Cargo' appeared in *Acumen*. 'CE' appeared in *Ambit*. 'Another Moment Like This, Please' first appeared in *The North*. 'Shoes' appeared in *Interpreter's House*. 'Suddenly Everything Speaks' and 'THEATRE STAFF ONLY' in *Orbis*.

'Arch of Defeat' was published in *Orbis* as 'Stopping in Traffic. Staring at Wellington.' 'Lonely. We can tell you.' was published in *The Frogmore Papers* with the title 'The Number 14 Bus.'

'Connected,' 'Intimissme' and 'Machine Upset' appeared in the Cinnamon Press Anthology *Reaching Out*.

'Sloane Square' was shortlisted for the Bridport Prize.

To J

i.

Connected

The buzz, vibration –
Who? Now? Why? Must.
Now – in my pocket.

Reach for it –
Nothing on, not there.
Phantom ring.

Intimissme

Two arms – plastic –
Tossed on a bed in the window –
The store dark and empty.

Looking back:
Mannequin, no arms, staring at the bed.

I stare, your young lover
Seeing you naked in the morning.

The brunette wears a dress.
The blonde, imitation fur.

A shopgirl dresses you
In a style you'd never wear.

I don't remember your dress
On the night we always said yes.

On the streets you forget.

You roll by – nice underwear.
The bus comes. There you are, rolling by,
Waiting for me. You don't blush.

I'm waiting for the next bus.
There you are on the bus, blushing.

My bus. There you are, rolling by
Between betting and beer.
I haven't changed. Have you?

(Where are you and
what are you doing?)

Machine upset,
Magic wand confused.
Pat down – nothing,
Chemical test – nothing.
They let me go through
Like I am nothing.
What did they miss?

(Don't call me. Text me.)

Bent over mobiles –
Fingers and buttons,
Ice gliding on ice.
Trashman sweeps
Between their legs.
Messages sent somewhere.
Can we speak like yesterday?

Sloane Square

These two smiling and striding,
Hugging longer than the bells.
Sisters? Classmates?
Is this their longest year of youth?

Jackhammers are attacking,
Taxis enraged.
Tourists on a bench flapping a map.
Red wreaths round the sword
On the cross of the cenotaph.
Venus pouring love out of conch.
I can just hear you, Chloe,
Over the cry of the fountains,
Screaming in cold water,
Laughing as I jump in
A spring pool in the mountains,
Our frigid skin tingling.
Is that you in the sports car
Spinning round the square?
Is this me, here, by the fountain
Happy in the spray?

The tourists now gone.
The friends are gone.
On the bench an Indian woman,
Her sari green as the plane trees,
Tapping her miniscule keypad,
Making mistakes like me.

Shoes

One shoe lying in the street.
Two tossed on the crosswalk.
More shoes leading to the bridge.
A path, a pattern, a confetti
Of lost, removed, discarded shoes –
Old pumps, new flats, heels, trainers,
Shoes without names, shoes I can't name,
Shoes made for the future, shoes soon
From the past, shoes like spring petals,
Broken canes, cracked bones, shoes
Wrinkled as skin, buckles twisted, straps
Torn and snapped, tongues dried up,
Shoes heading to the tunnel, marching
Across the square, strolling around
The arcades, pausing along the esplanades,
Running and darting and scuffling
Through an alley to a dead-end pile.
Someone there, in shoes,
Looks back as if to find where are they –
The barefoot people – and follows
A fading footfall down the ramp
To a river of shoes carried off.

The ad, sign, shoes, next street,
Your lobster walking the leash.
They say don't be ridiculous –
We're not ridiculous. They say –
Suddenly everything speaks.

                                              (I'm lonely today.)

Lonely. We can tell you.
She talks. I'm anyone.

He screams at the driver.
'Why won't you listen to me?'

They don't know where.
You tell the best way you know.

We want the bus to go faster.
I try to read the words.

We have much to do.

(Stopped in traffic. Staring at Wellington.)

Arch of Defeat,
We are building every day.
For centuries we never stop.
We build tall, we build wide
In the centre of our city,
In the bedrooms of our suburbs,
Where love wants softer pillows.
We build in halls of our universities,
Where young people always ask,
In the wards of our hospitals,
Where our doctors answer to death.

Visitors say why are you?
It's big enough? When will you stop?
No. Never. We are going to failure.
Otherwise we shall never stop.
How will you know when?
We shall never stop.

Conquerors demand legal reasons
Carved precisely in our arch.
They shake swords and axes,
Roar and throw our holy ones
In the bear pits to torture an answer
For a question they never accept.
They tear down our Arch of Defeat –
They raise an Arch of Triumph.
Slaves work quickly and afterwards
Burn with the plans and architects.

12

Shops are talking.
Do you think they're afraid
We won't come in and talk?
People are walking fast.

20 % off.
I'm full price –

50 % clearance.
I'm still here.

Total liquidation.
I walk faster.

Closed. For rent.
Where did I go?

Reduced

To a mountain of desire
Tumbling down into the sea.
The money flying to the stars
As the dresses drown.

Like a march, movement,
A protest for miles
Wide as trooping this hour's colours
And I'm shopping too.
I am one feeling. It's small. A flea.

Extra 30 % slashed.
I was too late. Final clearance,
But I already have.
Everything must go except
I'm staying here.
Am left behind staying here.
Only the solvent.

I got him a frame:
He'll spend years looking
For the right one.

Hush, I took you to Hush. (Don't tell anyone.)
The oysters tasted like her navel.
After lunch a drink at the CasBar.
Tall drinks as blue as her eyes.
Browse or buy afterwards.
(You'd both like that, wouldn't you?)
You karaoke like a girl you used to know –
You.

Skulls in the windows,
Skulls on his arms.
Skulls on your pillows.
Skulls are her charms.

I say death-wish.
'Oh, don't be serious.'
I have a skull in my head
Grinning back at you.

Here I am today –
Leather looks good:
Feel the spring
In these test steps.
The month. The season.
Next year. This year.
You'll have to take this off

The price,
The dress
Your head
And your heart,
The cover,
The cap,
The lid
On the Id.

And this was the video store
Boarded up now like a plague house.
All inside now. All the images.

Hi, how are you, Surgeon General?
Shopping. For what they don't have.

Hello, and you, Minister of Culture?
Returns.

We don't want here.
We could go to there
And not be. I don't know.
What would we be if we did?
What's that in the bag?

Returns.

Nobody in the supermarket
And it was 24/7.
Nobody in the offices
And the messages said soon.
No one in the tanks
And it was time to fire.
No one in one store
And it was time to buy.

I'm talking to you as I buy
The special ones here – the last ones here –
And feeling I'm talking to you here.

When I have time.
When I'm relaxed.
When I want to be
Tomorrow or today.
When you're gone.
The prices, I mean.

I love them closed,
Lit up like an aquarium,
Schools of fish flitting,
Colours spread out in rainbows,
Fishermen casting nets.
O the stores, the soul.

Double-decker,
Looking down,
Down to the people,
People marching
The grids of the city.
Looking down to
People like me.

Looking up.
Someone above, in a window,
Looking down,
Down at me
In a window.

In the rain we couldn't read the numbers
Or the bold names above.
We couldn't see displays or signs.
We were walking towards our footsteps
And they said 'Follow.'

.

I saw your name

spelled with stones on the slope of a teenager's hill,
tagged along rainy highway sound barriers,
scrawled on an overpass of the M something,
stencilled in Arial across the side of a moving van,
postered and tattered on plywood walls tilting
and shaking in wind the building site summoned.
I saw your name on the door of my dented car,
on my front door, in my mail and messages;
in the eyes of cameras and jumbo-mumbo screens
calling for attention and love I saw your name.
You were canvassing every street, contemplating
a blue-plaqued passage where you lived as no one.
Up below skyscrapers, along the Embankment
when unoccupied night people rise and crawl,
I saw you stabbing your stubby brushes, marking
the red and black indelible, hissing the sprays.
A vintage biplane, groaning a mechanical mantra,
trailed smoke, writes a sweeping, disappearing script.

ii.

Cash machine says no.

People behind me now jab –
The money arrives with a smile.
I am returning –

Cash machine says no.
These numbers are correct.
Cash machine says call number.

Cash machine empty.
Wallet empty.
Banks, countries empty.
How soon is when?
White, grey, black:
The lights are changing.
Take me there, cab driver

Because it's a different way.
Because I've been taking the same way –
Because I haven't gone this way.
Because how would I know if it was the way?
Because I can go back to the same way?
Because I don't mind becoming the diversion.

I know I have the heart of an explorer

Perspective of a wheelchair:
Buildings at twisted angles
As twisted as my legs
And I'm always searching
For Himalayas I can't hike,
Channels I can't swim.
I dip my toes in another ocean.
Dolphins are riding the waves.
If I could ride dolphins.
The guide books I'm reading.
My dog-eared chair.

A tiny entry

Flats above.
Chiropractor below.
He sleeps in a chair
Each time I go –
A baggy leftover face,
Twisted putty slouching
And dressed as tweedy
As an old gentleman.
Today he mumbles hallo
Slow and fading
As that shrinking bird
In the cage in Cairo.
He's gone tomorrow.
I don't notice.

Hello, Doctor

No, I'm not. Yes, I am.
(Bare branches lash against the window,
Whipping the glass case prisoner.)

Sometimes. Higher and lower.
(The branches coming to life,
Starting to bud and bloom.
Pink against a grey sky.)

Right there. I'm awake at night.
(High twittering of the orioles
In the vast green oak tree
And a plane silver as the sun.)

What if I don't? I can.
(Hard leaves fall onto frozen ground.)
My time's over. Someone else waiting.

My butcher

On his bike delivering
A wave to me and morning.
Both of us here. Still here.

Menus, menus,
New tastes from the sorcerers.
Interiors by Anno Mirabilis.
Waiters who are as gracious
As beautiful servants for a god.

The pharmacist can read it,
Hurried pinched letters –
Hoodoo he can decipher
In the face of worry.
A memory of every time
He translates love.

Spontaneous. No.

More a deliberately unplanned,
A trip to the desert when the sand blooms.
The tourist knows where he's going.
I walk around the world –
Every life I never lived
I can remember sometime.

Of course I am. He goes from 1 to 100 in zero!
Anything you tell him to do!
He's always screaming we're ruining his life,
We're the king and queen of always right.
Yes, you would raise your voice –
He's the riot and we're the bullhorn.
It's over so quickly – thunderstorm in summer,
Winter warming, melting to tears.
I wish he wasn't. I wish he could.
I can't believe what he says,
How he treats us – equals he doesn't respect.
Yes, he does. A lifetime in two minutes.
I have never more loved, never loved more.

Hearing You

Father and son and shadows
Striding the twilight street.
'When you have a plan in life...'
Their steps leave the shadow
For road construction ahead.

THEATRE STAFF ONLY

The costumes done for the day.
The props resting silently.

The stage black —
An understudy rehearses the dark.

'Whether it is nobler...'

The high age of eloquence
Dressed in horse hair,
Eating from a trencher,
Sleeping on a straw mat,
Waking to the wolves,
Smelling of chamber pot,
Dirty as a tramp,
Heaving on the chainmail,
Riding to Bloodingate,
Slashing off an arm,
Disemboweling a brother,
Draw-and-quartering prisoners,
Praying to God for the victory.
In our warm wired room,
Turning on the comfort,
Taking a bath in the jetstream,
A man and woman speak
A few thudding grunts.
Hamlet ageing. The skull.
An astrolabe on the table.
Necromancy on the chair.
Ophelia drowning in the tub.
I like your red-red hair.
I can imagine our skulls.
Channel 4. An autopsy.
Russian Roulette Live.

It's time. Check messages:

'…hope in a great man's memory…'

Stagelights switched off.
Actor wobbles away.
Ice cream stains on the seats.
Maybe in the morning
A script tonight.

Looking through the bars. The same picture:
A teenage girl, an elderly soul with a cough
Both with a view and an iron gate.
The long private lawn. The order of the path;
Freshly raked gravel and gold earth.
The placement of benches and flowerbeds,
Daffodils rising again, unfolding,
And the disheveled hearts of violets.
A place, though, you'd want less lonely.
No Adam and Eves of urbanity here
On the finest day ordered in the catalogue.
No children flying on red wooden swings
Or Gran tending the bees, couples picnicking.
Empty today, beautiful, and empty every day
As if no one dared approach a delicate ornament.
A fear even the most graceful ballerina will break
Everything here into lost time and place.
A place you'd have as your soul's mate,
If open to other dancers from the waiting list.

I took mine twenty years earlier.
The square in the fall of imagination.
Spring in November. Greening light
That said, 'Step inside. You'll never age.
You'll have time for warmth, for sun.
Hope is always here. Joy never goes.'
She always looked twenty in my picture.
I was a hundred and five lives away.

(Where are they?)

In a garden

When I catch you
(says the mother to her son)

You won't catch me
(says my lover to me)

I've locked the garden,
I've hid the key

Give it to me
(says my love to me)

I caught you
(laughs the mother to her son)

She grabs my arm,
bites my hand for the key.

Even if I had the key,
Even if I could let you in,
Even if this were our garden,
Our place alone,
I'd have to lock the gate.

A streetcleaner,
Sky uniform, sky glasses. Sky eyes?
See him floating into the sky
And disappearing blue on blue.
He's tethered –
A teddy bear tied to the handle.

Dragon School

Out the large gothic double doors,
Down dirty red medieval steps
Onto swoosh-swoosh-honk-'Excuse me,'
'Excuse me'-some-of-them-smiling,
Some-of-them-in-the-screen,
Most dodging you-in-the-way streets.

You are the tail of the Dragon teacher
And not yet growing your scales,
And the fledging dragon can't fly,
Caution clutching heavy hands,
Heads fixed as guards on parade.

A boy and a girl at the back laughing,
Looking up at neglected sky.

Here's the street leading
To the other street.
There's a sign leading to the sign.
No sign. Here's the street.

The walk a museum of shops,
The shops today, the familiar artifacts –
The remains of a city, unearthed.
I did one last year. Pompeii.

This street curves.
No reason it shouldn't be straight.
The surveyor made a mistake,
Made one on purpose.
Thank you, elegance.

As do the streets
The store has a sign
And I'm not lost
Asking the direction
And not listening
On the way to Hurry.

Are you sure, cut-through?
Maybe the next one.
Stick to the straight ones.
A bet on hurry lost to lost.
Hurry up now, short cut:
Footfalls of darkness laughing.
No one else. Stupid me.

The long way was shorter.
Destination, didn't mean to hurry you.

You read. In the headlines.
I never know how long.
Maybe there's a passion.

He's The Man

He's the man with no arms.
He's always walking fast,
A dash, a blur, quick-eyes-behind-head.
The hands, shirt and jacket pinned up
Like a man in a straight jacket.
He's the man and he's married
To the woman keeping pace.
Her love hasn't slowed the race
Through a course of bowed stares.

Mr. Inkin

Silver hair slicked back in the fashion of his youth.
Yellow sweater, green striped shirt, collar upturned
As if he were sailing with the wind, not against it.
He calls hello across the street and wall of cars,
Strolling this morning, every morning
To the newsagents and three papers.
A story to tell Rajan at the register.
Then looking back up his terraced street.
Perhaps Café Blanc later, get a treat.

Sleeping on the sidewalk.
Sifting through the trash.
A human on four legs
Sniffing and tugging at my legs.
I have a dog at home.
Standing upright, trying to walk.

(Funny, I was feeling happy today.)

When you're teetering down the aisle
Like a spilling crate of Spanish onions.
You were swaying and stumbling with me,
The bus jerking, irritated by too many stops
And daytripping cargo dumped on hard seats.
You with your pumps pumping the pedal –
Grinning in the tunnels of Switzerland,
A careening train through the mountains,
A hydrofoil to Malmo, tempestuous plane ride
In our holding pattern, airport-sized anticipation
Now like the last time must have belly-laughed.
Must Office-to-Office. Hurry The Hurry-Up.

C.E.

Spires ringing out of tune
Somewhere in the skyline.
When they were skyline
Ill-fed peasants,
Ill-clothed, ill-shod,
Feet numb in winter,
Senses delirious in summer.
And the artisans –
Rough tools,
Ropes and wooden scaffolds.
And centuries crept
Along with plans.
And generation to generation
Endured collapses and fires,
Falls and fatalities.
And the logical impossibility
Of miraculous building.

At the front of the nave
A white-robed choir outnumbers
Seven souls scattered
Among ninety-eight pews
A makeshift staff of grey heads
Flecked with clear-eyed blonde boys
Singing medieval.
The bishop's burly voice
Ringing loudest.

And louder than chatter
Of crowds roaming the aisles,
Their shorts and T-shirts,
Sandals and sneakers,
Backpacks like hunchbacks.
Sweating, they stop

And listen ten seconds
To the foreign sounds,
Words of frank love,
Notes of brittle faith,
And then are drifting
Across bright tiles
Painted as Eden.
Afterwards, lapsed,
Abstract as speed.

To find a quiet one there.
To sit down at the table outside.
To order a cup.
To be part of the setting.
It's been going on here
Since the setting.
When there's time.

Centuries

We were next to it,
The robot eyes recording
Every potholed block
And stop to go.
We were there, we were
In the version until the next version.

(Are we in the next version?)

When you dared not look back
It was me following you into spring.
The people were blooming.
We were still winter. Persephone.

Mouth of the street
Swallowing our last light
Trying to escape
In a car racing the other way
Into deeper darkness.
Taillights and flashing lights.
Red lips and red lights.

(I don't know where you are.)

Between dark sky
And dark land
A streak of red light.
The skies in us still burning.

Watching a helicopter.

iii.

Text? Call? Where?

My appointments.
Their appointments.
Clouds of abbreviation.
I lost you in the menu.
I didn't see your message.
I didn't hear your call.
I'm lying. It's the truth.

The code doesn't work –
Count the digits:
Number missing a number.
Catch the runaway number.
None of them open the lock.
Maybe if you were someone else.
Your neighbour with the bloodhound.

The Organizer
Ministers and Administers
Councils and Offices
The Square in the City
The City of the Organizers
The Country of the Councils
The Answers for the Questions
The Questions to the Answers
The Plaza with the Statues
Of Gods laughing in unison.

'No. Yes. Never. I can't hear you!
Are you a real person today?'

The voice coming faster,
Approaching and the street
Turning when I'm turning.
Louder, closer, here.

My old number's ringing
And when I answer
The same voice is approaching.
Who's that now?
Not the right beep.
The ring sounds different.
Don't you know me?
Don't I know you?
Don't say me.
I'm going to save that one
In case I don't need it.
It will be stored in air
And found when erasing.
I will save the laughter.
Maybe you'll cry.
In here I can save it.
The memory I had.

Any history?

Of joy? Laughter? Jumping
From the cliff into the puddle
Of contentment or sparks?
Of sunbathing naked?
Of rolling in snow?
Of songs in the bathtub?
Of desire on the treetops?
Of top hats? Dreams?
Sitting in a garden listening to traffic?
Of keeping a diary?
Of not watching? Of not buying?

Are you?

Mother's name, favorite place.
(When I was young.
When we were young
And leaping out of trees
Into a bonfire of leaves.)

Address. Post code.
Last four digits.
First and third digits.

(Where are you?
I've been there.
No. I'd like to.)

Next four digits.
Second and fourth digits.
(You'd like the coral reef.
I hear it's almost gone.)

Are you completely satisfied?
If there's a position open.
If there's enough allotment left.

I want my password
To leave this locked up state,
Buy my ticket when there's room,
Learn where I am going,
What other numbers I need
To leave numbers.

I want my password
To tell you who I am,
Allow myself entry to the system,
Open the gate to my departure,
Dive through the portal
And return dripping-wet new.
This message has been a message.
Customer Procurement Manager,
The water is freezing. *Whoo*!
Can't find a towel. Can't find number.

Data Protection Alert.
Go ahead – take my name,
My passcode, my passport,
My favorite place, my life –
You really think they're me.
You really think you are?

Breaking news

We watch the words.
We read the images.
A rope to the sky.
The last moment smile.
They were beautiful.
They were falling –
The people on the bridge.
Bombs accidently
Bombing the bridge.
They were all falling,
Falling and screaming
Off the bridge.
The words. The images.
A swoon to death.
They were beautiful,
Beautiful as outrage.
Do you have anything ugly?

I don't know why I looked back.
I don't know why I walked back
And peered in the window like an expert
Expecting to find a lost masterpiece
In a shop selling folding desks and campaign chests.
She was riding a hackney,
A lady in a straw bonnet,
The sky as hazy as the style
Meant to be more real from a distance
But no more real than the clouds.
I don't know reasons. I looked back
At this ordinary scene of driving a horse
Down a country path on an impressionistic afternoon.
I could say something smart
About the swirl of the clouds,
The indeterminate light of the sky,
The smallness of horse, the hackney,
The flowing dress of the lady,
The whisper of savagery from wild fields.

The Day War Was Declared

I want, I will sit in this square for a moment.
  (Don't forget your appointment.)

I do, I will have time for a pastry in the sun.
  (Don't forget where you're going.)

First I will walk around this dirty bench.
  (Don't forget your timing and your part.)

I must talk to the director about this world.

It was a happy day for us

We asked them who they were.
They had to tell us, prove it,
Know their names and codes,
Remember their hiding place
And how many square feet.
They had to answer every question,
The same ones they ask us
Every session without mistakes.
It is their turn, their secrets.
An honest reply assuming a lie.

(Text me. I've got news.)

The letters slow my rush.
They are lines and circles
The hieroglyph squad will have to decipher.
They are letters before words,
Before you wanted words to be messages:
Clear. Sensible. Messages.
I'm going swimming today.
The water is floating through me
Like light through a sponge.

(Text me again.)

I'm sorry you couldn't understand
I've lost hope in speed
And the tap-tap-swoosh.
No more racing blank spaces.

My fingers crooked as crooks.
I'm no shepherd.
Where are the directions?

Which way are you?
The right or wrong
Or the doesn't matter.
The coordinates of perception,
The district of final origin.
Plot me somewhere
I can still find you.

(Test me. I mean text me.)

A maze

On a bus watching me walk.
On the street calling you
Waving from a window –
In Holland Park during a tulip day
I see me kissing you
While I'm tying my shoe.
A clocktower. A watchtower.
The hours are watching.
Where are the judges?

Driving with fury of Furies.
Walking with the speed
Of those heel-toe athletes
Late, looking for the race.
You didn't see me coming,
Waiting, watching when
You turn and dive
Into the shopping bags.

On bus, squeezed into tube.
In taxi, in chair.
At meeting. For greeting.
On trip. In their chair.

Watching me go by.
Blur on the bus.
See-through reflection in window.

Someone and the mannequins.
They look better than us.
Passing cars and I'm gone.

You've been there. I have not
Climbed your marble stairs, bowed at gold shrines,
Decamped in cool blue riads,
Wandered jasmine gardens
In desert night and dreamed
Of conquest, peace, our own palace.

Morocco, I haven't been there -
That white beach. Haven't met that bronze woman,
Her eyes daring me to laugh at my reflection.

'Morocco. Why Not Now?'

'58 Dead In Cargo...'

Inspectors at Dover found them
Slumped behind crates of tomatoes,
Suffocated in the airtight freight-hold
On the hottest weekend of the year.
Five hours across the Channel, the truck's
Refrigeration unit switched off....
The BBC and Independent tell me
They died dreaming a better life.

I think we all know a better life –
I see it shining on the screen.
Sometimes, locked in the freight-hold,
Trapped with ash-heaps of longing,
We die dreaming a better life.

On time for the big building.
Walking to the corridor.
Walking to them. Talking to them
Talking like me talking to me.
Looking for the address.
Finding the dress.
Thinking of you thinking
Where you are now.
On the grass. In the sun.
On the elevator. On your own.
Someone smiled today.

(Who? Where? It's never lovely in Camden.)

Avoid the soup kitchen market,
The throwback black T-shirts
And go back there in the rain
When the market's closed
And the streets are lit like gloom.
It's really lovely in Camden.
You can see the Japanese Popstars
At their no invitation only secret show
And back at the afterparty upstairs
The promoter who never showed
You how to talk art to smoke –
He's here to instruct you.
I saw us at the Roudhouse as support.
But you weren't there to listen.
I went to his funeral, crowds chanting,
'Camden, Camden, Camden Again.'
You, careening round the bend of
Low expectations of Camden,
Taxied back to a garden flat
You don't call Camden
To a room you used to believe
Would keep you out of Camden,
Where you never go, where we are.
Do you know anyone here?

We live here now

We squeeze in the clothes.
Our pictures crowd the walls.
Drawers and cabinets stuffed
And too jammed to open.
Stumbling over narrow floorboards.
The attic refuses new donations.
The car on the street wants a garage.
Another car and two discontents
And the usual expectations for
Treasures, souvenirs from the dead
And living packed in storage boxes,
The scorching roar of airplanes
Somewhere past the highway,
Byway, motorway, flyway.
Give them away. Get out, they say.

I came to a book
Lying on the sidewalk,
A dead fish splayed open
Sculpted in an agony of rigor mortis
And somehow balanced upright,
An accordion stretched for a mournful tune.
It was big, a giant book as big as a bench,
Hard as a bench, and my legs were hard
From going back before getting there.
I sat down slowly, at first not sure
If the book like a bench would hold me
Like the ball and chain holding the book.

I tried to read the pages underneath –
Blank or faded pages that wouldn't turn.
I thought of inscribing the *Desiderata,*
But I needed a master's chisel
And had no training in masterwork,
Only a feeling I couldn't quite feel
Of sitting on a hard blank book
With pages that wouldn't turn,
While in a crowded room I'm talking
To you who had read the book
Too heavy now to carry.

Joy when
He kicks a ball into the sky.

Joy after
A ball enters a picture of the sky.

(My phone's dying.)

Range Rover, Range Rover pull over for me.
Your children are wailing, you're texting the sea.
Your phone's on caffeine racing XXE.
Range Rover, Range Rover don't run over me.

You're always tailing me,
Giving me a little tap of it,
The hunting horn in traffic.
Push on your pedal.
Hurry me to your pulse rate.
You don't like it, do you?
Behind you, me going faster.
Me nudging you at Go.

In cars complaining
It's never been today like this.
We are in our way.
You and I are traffic.

Don't look at them. Their anxiety
Spewing out the exhaust pipe.
Get there without time.

If we don't work together,
If we don't go to the same church,
If we don't belong to the same gym,
If our kids don't go to the same school,
I'll talk to you maybe
Once a year, my friend.

I Still Love The Sound

The swoosh of a rocket faster than space.
How the distance evaporates...
My message to you.

Deleting you

I remember how you took me in
When the streetcleaner seemed a friend.
I met your friends and you recommended me
Like a new commodity to believe in.
I remember that you listened
And patched me with a future
That would make the past someone else.
You gave me your car to drive,
Invited me to your family.
I played uncle with your children
And flirted with your young wife.
The house vibrated with the music
Of our dancing words. And you,
You made those remarks.
The floor opened and I dropped down a chute.
I don't know where. It was your laugh.
I remember you laughing as I fell.

There you are, Antonio,
Standing outside Antonio's.
No puffing today.
Watching cars crisscross,
Your red and white apron
How I know your name
A year before you nod.

Antonio crossing the street
Over the music, titles, credits
To the foreign newsagent's.
Visiting Raj. A smile,
A shrug, a cigarette.
Leaving with *La Republicca*
Folded like chars for the same seas.
The opening shot framed
Behind a stenciled window
Reading THE END backwards.
Waiting for the start to arrive.

Florence, once a ventriloquist
Of regulars and strangers,
Squeaks a rag over wet tables.
Vincent cranks the striped awning,
The sweeper sweeping the last
Of the discarded scripts.
Over stoical rows of shops
That wake with the first grey
And open doors to us
Pan to men in suits in the sky.

Had they been up there yesterday,
Another day, another decade?
Method actors pacing the roof,
Looking down and pointing up
As if naming the clouds
For people who were dead
And watching us set the scene,
Watching as if they pitied
Our loafing and scurrying
Our prows against the wind.

I never noticed streetlamps
Looking down like cameras.
The necks of swans, the eyes
Of sunflowers, lights on you
Looking through a tired lens.

On this pale white street
Straight as a pale white street
A house with blue window frames,
A blue hard to describe
By the novice designer
Except as a bright, friendly blue
Washed out by the liquid crystal
Of my washed-over eyes.
Who lives here now?
Try less screen time.
Look around neighborhood.
Remember sky.

Another moment like this, please:

Drops of light
snowing through slots
of the scaffolding.

Not knowing the season
and where and who
for one flickering stride.

The kids across the street.
On the same bus as ours.
We moved in. They were there.
Our windows aligned,
Our shadows aligned.
We said hello. We never met them.
Anger is like this.

Oh, the man without arms –
Carrying a tie back from the cleaners.

If I saw you again

Do you mind me asking, 'Are you crying?'
No, I never think crying's about me.
You don't have to apologize for your eyes.
I traded them for an empty room
When they were sleeping in shifts
With the husband who stole the thief
Of your happiest life. To meet yourself
As someone else you didn't know
Would admit trespassers and priests
Into the lilac garden of your next bed
In which you forgive trespassers.
The confessor said you decided
On an Asia rock garden
Instead of perennials in Patagonia.
I'm fading from the geography,
You're cringing behind cities
I approach like lips on your coffin.
I don't know when you are dying.
Regrets are the reunion
Of mirrors and one-way tickets.
On the street try to keep the memory
Of your next life from burning
With the letters the firemen couldn't save.
I took the bullet train to Central Station.
The saints of New Orleans –
They were marching as I danced
To your favorite song, one I remembered
As the only note I sang to you,
The tune visiting the grave of our youth.

Ringtones

They're ringing and flashing.
(Why are they flashing?)
I was the slave,
Slave until I realized
I could ignore you,
Let messages pile up
Like trash in the alley.
My eyes and my soul
Tired of living fast.
Now I'm weapon.
Photos, library.
They are mine,
The information,
Inventory, report.
My record of this.
Now I'm the weapon
Alone like a gun.
How much data in my soul?
How much storage left?

She's dressed for a funeral of ants.
His ear candy's getting fatter.
You have to believe evolution goes backwards
To understand what they're grunting.
You slump like a shopping bag
Carrying returns without receipts.
Now you're an out-of-fashion model
Begging for click-click-flash.
You haven't loved since your mother died.
You wish that your father would die.
The rattle of his career. The dimming of his mind.
Now you haven't loved since she left you.
Is that your choice? You horrible me.

I walked through the courtyard
Under the spray of fountains
Towards the darkness.

I walked through the silence,
Through too much light.
I did not miss them.

I walked up a green hill
For a view of the city
Welcoming the darkness.

I walked through the city at dawn.
I walked back into the darkness.
I did not miss anyone. I did.

(Do you wish you could walk?
Throw out the angry horn?
Have eyes instead of mirrors?)

What if you are always alone?

Seven stories up
Just the structure
Open as a viewing deck,
A high dive for the brave,
A ten-story picnic,
The workers on lunch
With the short-sleeved sun,
A tanned breeze drying their temples
Before walls and windows arrive.

And the scaffolders –

Climbing any house,
Clanging the joints.
The high wobble.
Watch for them falling

On you, on me.

Banging the pipes,
Banging the brackets.
Clinging to masts,
Sailing over chimneypots

Over me, over you.

The planes line up for the sky.
The sky open for flight.
Remember when we would disappear?
Only the clouds would know.

Crow on a streetlamp.
Black against white sky.

Didn't see you, crow.
Didn't see you, streetlamp.
Cyclops eye hanging from sci-fi skeleton.

Don't know why I looked up.

Hallo. Who are you?

I keep getting these strange messages
About angry cars and history?
Can you check your history?
Maybe it's some kind of system error.
I hope I'm not seeing something I shouldn't.
This isn't some kind of crazy code
And being the mistaken recipient puts me in danger?

I keep getting these strange messages about angry cars and
history.

Don't worry. It's a language,
A cryptic code, a Coptic inscription,
A clue, a guess, a hint, a hunch
That whatever we mean by strange
Is a place to start a new colony.

And I'm Walking

And white pillars with numbers rise and fall.
And white pillars with numbers rise and fall.

iv.

Her face. Face on the cover.
Who is she?

Her smile, smile on you.
What is she?

Her eyes, eyes on the billboard.
Must she?

She must be famous.

Trading As Usual

Man in the corner shop.
Decades of I will. I will I am.
Everyone his friend.
Delivers 4AM papers,
Makes the change,
Credits their accounts,
Smiles at their children.
But you remember.
Not my first country.
Not their complexion.

Benches round a tree
In the allotment of grass,
One tree and four benches
Staring at the tree.
It flowers. The branches spread
Over the benches. The leaves fall,
On the heads of the sitters
Sitting alone with the company of silence.
The tree will be here tomorrow
And after they've lived.
It might die first and will after
The storm, Dutch Elm, Tableau Construction.
A government decree agrees.
You whom I don't know looking
At the tree are four thousand years today.
Someone will be looking tomorrow.
The roots, the green and gold and bare.
The bare and bud and green.

.

Strange Bud

She's naming the tree with small leaves,
A strange bud she knows,
How it tests the climate, blooms and fades.
A greyed woman spinning her wheelchair
Under half-green hints of exotica.
The sky is grey as street grit.
The woman touches an overhanging branch
As if remembering the Latin name.
Where she used to shout 'Go!'
She races metallic shadows to the sun.

A boy like a torpedo scooters by. 'I was dead.
I was dead like that one and after I died...'

In the airport her silver-haired gentleman,
Fixing the knot in her paisley scarf,
Fingers red and green buttons
On the stopwatch he once ran against
In woods tangled with trails and overgrowth.
She is swinging from the lounge furniture,
A pale white egg designed by love
For birches scrolled up for the winter.

Recall crawling long arms of an American oak
And falling into pyres of crackling leaves.
Sharp edges stick to our wool sweaters.
Burrs we pull out like truant monkeys.
Grooming each other in African sun.

She was veering, she was tilting,
She bent like a broken branch,
Walked like a warped board.
She was talking to ducks and children.
'A new season!' I heard her say,
Catching a falling cherry petal
Presenting it like a gift to a child
Eyeing her and then the nanny.
I love the seasons changing
And she was talking like laughter
That seemed to help her walk.
Well, I noticed that she was beautiful:
Long brilliant hair and a tanned grace,
Her oval face as smooth as a cameo
In the window of a junk shop.
And I could say I would love her,
I would walk with her unashamed
Of branches and lonely laughing.
I would be proud of showing I loved
A strangely broken creation.
And I should say I am lying:
It was embarrassing – her bent body,
Her ignorance of knowing how
To leave us to this day of beauty.

I'm Sorry To Tell You This

(You shouldn't have told me this.)

There is a penalty for misuse
I love you let's not meet
Sometimes you need glue
When faces are broken
It used to be my worst feature
I love you let's not meet
The next stop is mine
And yours, yours and yours
There is penalty for misuse
I love you let's not meet

Toujours 24

In here I'm Dear.
Out there I'm always leaving.
In here I'm arriving –
Tomorrow I don't see her
Or next year twenty times.
They used to know me here.
They don't know her.
Breakfast on a throne
Any hour with Louis Quatorze.

Foch 1851-1929

Who leaves the wreaths?
Who is this straight-back rider
You can google for extra points?
An officer and a gentleman neglected
And gazing at a corner of Victoria Station.
Prizefighter eyes. Pride and a bad view.
I don't know who leaves the wreaths.
Passing is asking a question.

The dates,
Not when he died.
When he lived.
It's March, cold this March.
The gardener says, 'Late.
The bulbs are late.'

Where do you come from?
How long will you stay?
Today you know my order
In the order I want.
Today you understand me
And I ask you your questions.
Tomorrow I'm here and you're gone.
And I'm gone too.

Goodbye, Foreign Waitress

Now I am here long enough –
This street I'm crossing,
These stores and the station
Like others in other lives.
I'm glad I'm home before dusk.

You are again. Again
In the pages, on the news,
Stepping out of the car,
Smiling at the cameras,
Waving goodbye to Analise,
Sitting in the photo booth,
Reading with your sunglasses
A one-page synopsis.
Have you seen me?
I had a mention here,
I almost made it there.
It was close. I'm getting there.
(No point in giving up now
Or what could I say then?)
And there you are again
When I'm close to almost.
I want you to see me.
Who is it you want seeing you?

A woman setting the table in a dim front room.
A man at his desk in white light.
Blue light kids playing games.
A head like a lightbulb looking out.
The blurred flicker of a passerby.

'Excuse me. Is that you or me?
Are you that real person I see?
I met magicians at the party.
They change faces and you can't see.

Oh, I'm sorry. I bet you are
Sad. The love, the houses, confirmation.

Enjoy yourself. Pretend. Fool everyone.
Goodnight, whoever you are.'

At the fundraiser

The fire put out, the smoke didn't rise
High enough for us to see.
The ambulance arrived with a flat –
The police came too late to care.
I haven't seen you very much at the party.
They want me to give lots of money.
How much does that question cost?
You will have to borrow the answer.
If the interest is too high,
We'll call in the militia.
The war was like a peace treaty:
Both sides agreed there were both sides.
Children were laughing at the trapezoids.
I was too backdated to understand the subtext.
Under the tornado is where I kept the words.
They are flying away to Mauritius.
Some broken into prehistoric rants.
Some words melting in the sun.
I'm looking back at my lost adjectives.
Can I borrow one for the era?
No, I have too many to spare
And you must name one isotope
Separating love from uranium.
And tell me the difference between
Now catastrophe or if apocalypse.
I was dancing in the beginning of Act I.
In the second I closed the curtains
And tripped the trapdoor:
The audience disappears into the ending.
The ballerinas escape through the skylight.
On the roof they pirouette for the birds.
Without a choreographer they didn't fly.
I learned it was more real on film.
Have you seen the movie about the script?
No, it didn't respect history either.

At the elephant factory

We're making them again.
Not like before.
No tusks. No hunters
In theme parks. Resorts
Where they used to live.
Everyone loves them.
Except for the shipping.

Any questions for Jane?

Projected outlook.
Impact on us.
European outlook.
Impact on us.

China, The Middle East, timber.
Portfolio invested to take advantage.

Uncertainty of the undervalued stocks.
General mood of city,

The world, the firm.
Impact on us.

(Tell them my concerns.)

Have you ever asked a question
And didn't understand the answer
And they may not have understood
What they said entirely
But that was all right with them?
Yes, that is what it feels like
When you're outside the money.
And we're there to help you help us
Know each of us who might help us
Be the one who helps us
Meet us with the money and power
Who can help us with the power and money
And you would still like us
Because like us you are interesting people
And we are us too. In the bathroom
Art Forum for us, anti-depressants for you.

(I'm late. Are you early?)

I'm out of range.
I'm in a meeting of them,
Women and men.
My battery's low.
My machine's really slow.
Experts are listening
And I'm lying now -
Lying in the bluegrass
Outside the time of day.
I'm looking at mountains.
The snow that's left
And the sun which melts.
Dissolve, dissolve.

(It's 5:30)

I'm here. Come out.
CCTV Cameras in Operation.
Did you get my message?
The sign says Refusal Often Offends.
Now I'm here. Where are you?
Diversion. Leave me alone.
Priorities Change Ahead.
No, I won't.
CCTV in operation.
Leave me alone.
Did you get my last message?
The signal is weak.
Await Help.
The signal is weak.

(5:45)

5:30. 6:15. Time for love
And there was a line.
(For a peek at the artist
Mounted under glass.)

They didn't have it so I
Went to And, And, And & And
(To the first page of twilight).

Rain. It was raining –
Taxi was crashing the other way
(En route to the streetlamps).

Well, I'm walking (the long way)
Past the gabled houses
On the quiet street we like.

Because when I'm with you
I'll tell you (if you want to listen).

Now I'm here. Where are you?
At an entrance. Where are you?
An exit. With a statue.
Of whom?
It's not a person.
Did you pay for the time yet?
Card was declined.
What happens next?
Visa. Where are you?
At an exit with a statue.
Of a person?

                                        (I can't find you.)

On train, on station
I couldn't find you
And almost sat down
With someone else
I thought was you.
She said, 'Oh.
I thought you were him.'

In housewares
I saw you going down.
You didn't see me.
Slowly, I turned around.

I was about to say,
About to say,
I know how it feels
Passing you by.

                                        (Was that you?)

Here in your network.
In my favorites.

In your messages
A second after you send.
Here in a buzz, a beep,
A ripple of our liquid screens.
Here in our history
Sent by the sky.

(My phone has died.)

Terminal,
Still bent over devices –
Fingers still frozen.
I've seen us before.
Lying like corpses
In a huge block of ice
Rescue workers hammer.
We slowly are melting.
I've lost all your messages.

(Do we need tickets?)

We are now ready,
Waiting for the journey,
When will it start
Where will it go?
Oh, we're already there.
Directions following us.
In a room of folding chairs
There are windows.

Arrival